ANDY ANT

by Pops Winky

PPH
Pacific Publishing House

ISBN 0-918872-01-4

Printing 1 2 3 4 5 6 7 8 9 0

Firdale was the largest ant town in the forest. The town gate, a
big old ant hill, stood among the trees not far from the crossroad.

It was the end of summer. Every ant hurried to fill the stores and warehouses before the rain and snow came.

The busiest ant in the town was the old gatekeeper. Every time an ant came in, the gatekeeper marked in a book whatever the ant carried — seeds, berries, or firewood for the winter.

Andy Ant lived in Firdale, too. He was always ready to help, but most of the time his help turned out to be very odd.

One day when he was in the forest, he saw a wagon piled high with firewood.

"I'll go help pull it," he thought, but he couldn't get to the ropes. "Oh, well, I'll help push." But there was no room behind the wagon either. Andy went around again and began pushing.

The trouble was that he was pushing the wagon backwards.

"Hey, you there," an ant shouted. "What are you doing?"

"Who, me?"

"Yes, you. You're holding us back. We've got no time for stupid jokes."

"I'm not joking," said Andy. "I'm trying to help."

"We don't need this kind of help. Get out of the way."

Andy stood aside and let the wagon pass. A little later he saw a lady carrying baskets of raspberries.

"Can I carry the baskets," Andy asked her.

The lady said, "I can carry them myself, thank you. But maybe you can help out at the warehouse."

Andy Ant thought it was a marvelous idea and followed the lady through the gate.

"Give us a hand, lad," someone said the minute he arrived at the warehouse.

"Sure," Andy said happily and helped getting a huge sack off an ant's back.

He looked around for more things to do.

"Gosh! What a busy place."

Everywhere ants were hurrying among the barrels and boxes and bins and baskets. Some were hanging ears of grass seeds from long strings under the ceiling.

"Oh, I know what I'll do," Andy thought. "I'll hang grass seeds. I love to climb ladders."

In a wink he was on his way up a ladder clutching an ear of grass seeds under his arm. But when he reached the top and looked down, he got scared. He was very high up and everything was so far below! He grabbed for the ladder, but he lost his balance and fell down headfirst smack into a barrel of raspberries.

Oh, what a mess! His head was in the barrel, his feet kicking the air. It took three ants to get him out, and when they set him down, they could hardly stop laughing. Andy Ant looked like a clown painted bright red.

"I can't stay in the warehouse," Andy mumbled as he went to wash up.

But he didn't know what to do next. Outside, he saw a police ant and asked him where he could find a job.

"Well, now," the officer said. "Let's see. What can you do?"

"Pretty near everything."

"That's quite a lot, son," the officer smiled. "Have you tried the Mushroomery? It's a good place. My cousin works there."

"The Mushroomery! Why didn't I think of that? Thanks an awful lot." And in the same instant Andy was on his way.

What a place the Mushroomery was! Mushrooms of every shape and size were growing everywhere, and among them ants were busy raking, digging, or harvesting mushrooms.

"Boy, I just love it," Andy cried with excitement and stepped off the path. "First of all, I've got to find a shovel."

He found a green garden hose on the ground. "I think I'll water mushrooms instead." He found the valve and turned it.

Somebody began shouting from behind a huge mushroom. "Turn off the water! Turn off the water!"

Andy, in his hurry, turned the valve the wrong way. He was still busy with it when the chief gardener appeared, soaking wet.

"Who are you," he demanded furiously, shaking a bony finger at Andy. "What are you doing here?"

"I'm looking for a job, sir."

"A job! You're lucky you don't work here. Because I'd fire you right now. Get out of here."

He was still wiping his face when Andy left the Mush-roomery.

"I'm good for nothing," Andy Ant thought sadly.

He stopped at a bakery looking at the cakes and the heaps of doughnuts in the window. He got an idea.

"Hey! This would be a great place for me." He gathered up his courage and walked in.

The baker came with a big apron tied around his belly.

"Sir, I'd like to work here," Andy said courageously.

The baker looked him over several times and asked if he liked cakes.

"Yes, sir, I do."

"How large a piece can you eat," the baker wanted to know.

"I don't know, sir. I've never had a piece large enough."

The baker nodded. "I can see that you're honest," he said. "You're hired, son, and you can start right now."

The baker gave Andy a jelly finger then sent him to the shop to learn how to make pies and pastries.

It was warm in the bakery shop from the row of glowing ovens. The bakers and apprentices were busy kneading, stirring, making cakes, putting loaves of bread in the ovens, or taking them out. Andy hardly knew what to look at first.

But after a while he got tired of watching. "I might as well get started," he thought.

He went to the back of the shop where the big wooden tubs stood. He wanted to make bread. He put some flour and salt and water in a tub, and added a whole box of yeast.

He was mixing and kneading happily when the yeast began to

work. The dough grew bigger and bigger. It swelled over the tub, spilled on the floor, and still it kept growing and growing. Soon the whole back of the shop was a mess of sticky dough.

"I've done it again," Andy sighed unhappily. He knew that he was through. He didn't wait to be sent away. He opened the back door and walked out quietly.

Not far from the bakery, Andy saw a sign at the entrance of a restaurant. It said, "BUS BOY WANTED. INQUIRE AT HEAD WAITER."

"At last somebody wants my help," Andy said.

Right away he walked inside looking for the head waiter.

"Sir, I saw your sign outside. I'd like to be the new bus boy. Can I start right now?"

The head waiter patted him on the back. "That's the spirit, my boy! That's what I like to see in a young fellow. Enthusiasm. You're hired, my boy. Keep it up and you'll make a fine waiter some day."

They gave him an apron and a cap, and showed how to set the table with plates and glasses and silverware.

At dinner time the guests began arriving. Waiters hurried in and out of the kitchen carrying trays of food and bowls of steaming soup.

"Get these tables set, my lad," the head waiter said. "We're expecting a party any moment."

Andy dashed in the kitchen and picked up a huge stack of plates. But in his hurry he forgot that one door was for coming in and the other for going out. And sure enough, he took the wrong door just when a waiter was rushing in.

Bang! Crash! Plates were flying all over the kitchen.

In a moment only broken pieces were left lying on the floor.

That was the end of Andy's job.

Andy Ant was on the street again. He was very unhappy.

"What should I do," he wondered sadly. "I'm just a plain good-for-nothing."

Then, suddenly, he heard the sounds of a trumpet. Then the booming of a drum. Then he heard a band playing a snappy tune.

Andy was standing right in front of the Music Hall. Very quietly he sneaked inside.

On the stage, the band was rehearsing. Andy stood at the back row listening eagerly, when the music suddenly stopped.

"Cymbalist! Cymbalist! You've lost your place again," the band leader shouted.

"But sir, you fired him yesterday," someone in the band said.

"So I did," the band leader stomped his feet. "Well, what are you waiting for? Get me another cymbalist."

"But sir, we have no other cymbalist."

At this moment Andy stepped forward. "Here, sir. I am your new cymbalist."

The band leader nodded. Andy took his place at the rear of the band, and picked up the two beautiful shining brass cymbals.

The band began to play, and every time the leader gave a signal, Andy struck his cymbals together.

When the music stopped the band leader stepped off the podium and rushed to shake Andy's hand.

"Bravo, bravo! You're the greatest cymbalist I've ever had," he said over and over, and he hired Andy right on the spot.

A week later Andy received a splendid uniform of red velvet with golden braiding all over the chest. He also got a tall cap with a smart black visor.

When spring arrived after the long winter, and all the ants
of Firdale went to the May Day picnic, Andy Ant was on the
band stand in his cap and red uniform, and he played his cymbals
so beautifully that everybody in Firdale was proud of him.